WALK LIKE A KING

THE YOUNG MAN'S
GUIDE TO CONQUERING
THE WORLD

JESSE A. COLE, JR.

Walk Like A King: The Young Man's Guide To Conquering The World.

ISBN: 978-0-9847798-0-2
Copyright ©2011 Maximize Your Greatness Publishing.

Published by Maximize Your Greatness Publishing

For Booking:
Booking@JesseSpeaks.com

Cover Design/Interior Layout: Dean Cole Creative
Photography by: LeoSage Images | www.LeoSageImages.com
Edited by: So It Is Written, LLC | www.SoItIsWritten.net

Printed in the United States of America. All rights reserved under International Copyright Law. No portion of this book may be reproduced or transmitted in any form or by any means, electronic or mechanical including information storage and retrieval systems without permission in writing from the publisher.

CONTENTS

INTRODUCTION 9

CHAPTER 1: LOVE 11

CHAPTER 2: INTEGRITY 33

CHAPTER 3: GOALS 37

CHAPTER 4: EDUCATION 49

CHAPTER 5: DETERMINATION 53

CHAPTER 6: PERSISTENCE 65

CHAPTER 7: SELF CONTROL 71

CHAPTER 8: K.I.N.G 77

CONCLUSION 83

WALK LIKE A KING

DEDICATIONS

To my parents Jesse and Dianna Cole, Sr., thank you for the life lessons, whether direct or indirect. You are a symbol of love and protection for me. You have given me wings to soar, but I will always remember where my home is. Without you, I wouldn't be who I am today and because of you I am able to walk like a king.

To Mr. Bobby Ray Ivory Jr., thank you for reminding me that I have what it takes to conquer the world. You are partially responsible for this book being created and because of your coaching/mentoring, I was able to gain a new level of clarity and self-awareness, allowing my ideas to breathe.

To The American Christian Writers, it is truly an honor to be associated with such a powerful group of people who are just as hungry as I am. I share your struggle as well as your milestones. Thank you for letting me be a part of your family.

To my wife Shaleena, you are more than my wife, friend, and vision manager. There is not enough space on this page to express how much you mean to me. The support and peace you bring to our home have created an environment that nurtures my endeavors. I appreciate you. I love you.

FOREWORD

The circumstances in America, perhaps the world over, concerning young black males is beyond crisis. I believe we are at the precipice of driving the presence of males to the point of irrelevance and impotency via the absence of a clear path to significance. In fact, I believe that there is a kind assault on what it truly means to be a man in any culture. Scripture teaches that "without a vision, the people perish" or cast off restraint. A man must see in his mind's eye what he can become before he can become it. Without the vision, chaos will ensue. Chaos will reign.

Many of our young men grow up without the benefit of having a strong, principled man in their lives and are forced to seek their identity in the unforgiving streets. This unguided pursuit leaves them filled with misinformation concerning the true nature of manhood. Thanks to men of valor like Mr. Jesse A. Cole, Jr., I am certain there is great hope to turn the tide favorably, not for black boys alone, but all young men who are in need of a proper path.

Mr. Cole has written a simple book to aid young men in becoming men of strength, high standards, and impeccable character. I believe that whether you're a single mom striving to ensure that your son(s) establish a sound basis for behaving as a man in this life, or a husband and wife seeking supplemental information to guide your son(s) journey into manhood, this book is for you.

Don't take my word for it; just turn a few pages and within seconds you will know that I have not led you astray. I know Mr. Cole to be a man of high standards and a man truly committed to seeing young men break disempowering patterns in their lives so that they may truly maximize their greatness. I believe this book should be a required reading in every junior high school in America. Well done, Mr. Cole. Well done.

Bobby Ray Ivory, Jr.
Author of *Power Up! Ten Points of Personal Power for Creating The Life You Want*
President & Founder of IvoryCoast Communications
www.IvoryCoastMedia.com

INTRODUCTION

Young man, if you are reading this right now, you are the reason why I wrote this book. I can identify with your struggle and I am familiar with your uncertainty and questions about manhood. I have heard your cries for understanding and direction, I know what your tears mean, and I even understand why you rebel at times. As I grow, one thing that I continue to be faced with is how the world views me as a man. As you mature, you will begin to have some of the same challenges.

As men, there is an undying passion to make the world see our heart, but there is a fear that they won't accept it as it is. We are faced with so many barriers that prevent us from truly being ourselves. Society demands that we be tough and protective, as well as kind and approachable. It wants us to be the bread winners as well as the spiritual nurturers of our families. We are expected to be everything to everybody, and look good while doing it.

Please don't be crushed by the pressure, and don't feel forced to prove your manhood to anybody. You are not obligated to be everything to everybody. Concentrate on getting to know yourself as a young king so that you can offer yourself to the world in confidence, not out of unnecessary obligation.

What you are about to read are chapters filled with attributes that I admire from strong men like Dr. Martin Luther King, Jr., my biological father Jesse A. Cole, Sr., and other great men who have invested time and wisdom into my life. I believe that these words can literally change your life for the better, if you allow it to. Once you finish reading this book, my desire is that you will continue to grow at a steady pace by exercising the principles of this book. As you develop, you will begin to see humanity respond to you with respect and reverence, and you will literally find yourself conquering your world.

CHAPTER 1

LOVE

GOD. SELF. FAMILY. COMMUNITY

When you hear the word love, what comes to mind? Do you see the face of that girl you would like to talk to or already have? Do you envision the embrace of your mother or grandmother? Maybe you are reminded of that special coach who helped you perfect your jump shot or the teacher who guided you through the tough areas of a particular subject in school. No matter what comes to your mind, I would be willing to bet that a feeling of comfort or security accompanied the thought.

Depending on who you are, your concept of love, what it means to you and how you receive it, will not be the same way someone else views love. Some people need to receive flowers to feel loved; others may require a series of kind words and affirmations in order to feel loved. But this one thing is for certain, we all need to feel loved. However, as we receive love, we must remember to give it as well. A wise man once said that, "It is more profitable to give than to receive."

So many people would rather receive gifts than give them, and I understand their point of view. It feels good to be catered to. It makes life a little more exciting when you can get everything you want. But here's the thing about love. Real love is demonstrated when it is given away and given unselfishly.

In order to walk like a king, there are certain aspects of love that you must address and embrace: your love for God, yourself, your family, and your community. Because of the magnitude and impact that each of these has on you and those around you, you must be careful to never taint them with selfish ambition. Let us examine them one by one.

LOVE GOD

The Bible tells us that God is love. Not only does it say that God is love, but we can actually see examples of His love since the beginning of time, and I am sure that His love will continue to impact people for years to come. He is the standard for love, He embodies love, and He is the ultimate giver of love. In order to understand how to love, you must use God as your example. His kindness, patience, tolerance, peace, grace, mercy, and discipline are all characteristics that make up the kind of love we are to express toward one another.

Don't get me wrong. I am in no way encouraging you to be one of those people who walk around hugging everyone and screaming, "I love you" every chance you get. But, what I am saying is that in order to have a balanced life, a life that is full of victories, a life that supports and promotes you as a KING, you absolutely must have the love *of* God and a love *for* God in your heart. Your love for God will open doors for you that your talent could never open. It has the power to create opportunities for you that no human being could ever produce. Don't be afraid to show it. Don't be too macho to express it. You cannot allow it to spoil on the inside of you. You must have enough courage to use it every chance you get. His love for you is so great that He offered His Son as a sacrifice so that you can have a better opportunity at life. He's not asking you to make that same type of sacrifice for Him, but I do think that He smiles when He sees you sharing His love with others.

LOVE YOURSELF

I love myself! Man, that felt so good. I think I need to say it again: I L-O-V-E MYSELF!!! The reality of that statement is powerful because I wasn't always able to say that. Not that I had a speech impediment or anything. I just wasn't confident enough to say it out of my mouth. When you look into my history, you will find that I was raised in a great home, with great parents who provided for their children in an awesome way. I got a good whipping every now and then *(most of them I deserved)*, but I wasn't abused and my parents came to 90 percent of my basketball and football games. Needless to say, I had a pretty good childhood compared to most of my friends.

So, you may be wondering what could have been the problem. If I had such a good life, why was it so hard for me to say that I loved myself? That is a great question. The short answer to that question is this: I had insecurities about my self-worth.

In elementary school, I was never the popular kid. The girls were not fighting for my attention *(that didn't happen until I got older)* and I wasn't the smartest kid in school either. As it relates to notoriety, I was kind of in the middle and it was easy for people to overlook me because I really didn't stand out. I considered myself a nice guy. I never caused any trouble. I did what I was asked to do and I never disrespected anyone. But, I guess that didn't matter to those who seemingly "mattered".

When I was in middle school, the only kids that got the attention were the ones who were super smart or the kids who got in trouble all the time. People like me seemed to get ignored a lot of the time and being ignored for no apparent reason was hard for me to deal with. What made my life even more complicated was that several of my friends were popular for different reasons, but it seemed like I never really fit in. It was kind of weird being on the inside, but feeling like you were on the outside. Sometimes I felt invisible and that caused me to feel like less of a person, which ultimately lead me to developing a habit of self-depreciation and a minor case of low self-esteem.

Once I finally made it to high school, I began to notice things gradually changing. I was still the same person that I was in elementary and middle school, but I began to focus more on building myself instead of expecting other people to build me up. I stopped feeling bad about not being popular and started to celebrate the reasons why people liked me. Like I said before, I didn't stand out, but people would always seem to come to me for advice about their problems. I wasn't the star basketball player, but my coaches always looked to me to lead our team. I wasn't the most prolific speaker, but I was always called on to give a word of encouragement to people who needed a boost.

Once I began to see this pattern, I decided to build on my good attributes and that was the start of me finding my identity as a man. During my senior year in high school, I received a basketball scholarship that allowed me to go to college for free. I was excited about this new opportunity because it was one of my goals since kindergarten, and my parents were excited because they didn't have to pay the thousands of dollars required to get a college education. Even though I was eager to go to college, I still had questions. I wasn't afraid to leave home and I wasn't nervous about the people I would meet, but I was unsure of how I would fit into this new environment.

One thing that helped me out was to think about the person that I had grown to be. I reminded myself of how I had grown from wanting to be in the popular crowd to being the one that the popular kids came to for advice. I recalled how other people depended on me to motivate and encourage them through their tough issues, and the words of gratitude I got once they felt better about themselves. I didn't need to change my personality just because I was in a new environment. I could just be me, love me, and everything would be alright.

As you mature in age and experience, you will learn that loving yourself is essential in your development as a man; however, not just any kind of man, but a man that adds value to the world. Adding value to the world means that the world is improving just because you are in it. Your presence makes such an impact that people seem to depend on you for all kinds of support.

This all sounds good, but in order to add value to the world, you have to love yourself first. There is no way around it. You can't give something you don't have. This means that in order to give love, you must already have it in your heart. There may be people you know who don't have a clue about how to add value to the world because they don't love themselves.

This can be compared to trying to pour a glass of milk from an empty milk carton. It is impossible! When you love yourself, the windows of opportunity fling open and present you with chances to make a positive difference in the world. You will begin to see mankind from a broader perspective, which will give you an advantage in helping to improve it.

I want to share with you several ways you can grow in your manhood and add your own value to the world through loving yourself. When you apply these steps to your life, you will begin to see yourself grow, and your footsteps will solidify your existence as you walk like a king.

Personal Hygiene

I learned early in life that personal hygiene is important. Your aroma says a lot about you. It lets people know that you either love yourself or hate yourself. In most cases, before people get a chance to hear your voice, they smell your aroma. You either make a good impression or a bad impression, but believe me; you *will* make an impression that will last long after your initial contact with them. Trust me; you will be labeled as a young man with bad hygiene if you don't pay attention to it. Personal hygiene consists of bathing daily, brushing your teeth daily, combing/brushing your hair, making sure your fingernails are clean, making sure your toe nails are clipped, and making sure that your skin is moisturized. It may seem like a lot to consider, but once you develop a routine of addressing your hygiene, it will become second nature and you, and everyone you come in contact with, will be grateful for the results.

I remember playing basketball and football in middle school, high school, and college. Those are some of the best memories that I have. Competing against other athletes who are just as hungry to win as you are produces an atmosphere that you just can't get anywhere else. It also produces perspiration. If you've played any sport, you understand that it can get sweaty and sometimes dirty during practice and game time.

After the game is when I smelled the results of my hard work. No matter if we won or lost our game, I always tried to make sure that I showered after my games. I didn't want to be the stinky kid on the bus ride home. Nothing is worse than sitting next to someone who has poor hygiene. It is one of those things that make life a little more uncomfortable for everyone who has to endure it. Honestly, who wants to sit next to the stinky kid? That is not a role anyone in their right mind wants to play.

Unfortunately, there are young men who have not paid enough attention to their personal hygiene habits. Some young men just don't care about it, while others just don't know how. I can't make you care, but I can show you how. Here is how you can make sure that your personal hygiene is on point.

Bathe Daily

The best way to ensure that you are on point with your hygiene is to address it before you leave your house in the morning. Yes, there will be times when you may be running late, those days when you are behind schedule and you have to be ready in an instant, so you may forget to wash up or shower, but this should never be your excuse *all* of the time. One way to make sure your body is clean in the morning is to take a bath or shower before you go to bed at night. When you shower or bathe before you go to bed, you won't have to feel rushed in the morning and it gives you more time to prepare for your day. Depending on how many people live in your house, taking a shower at night just might be the best option for you.

Also, try to find a soap or body wash that you like and a deodorant that smells good to you. If you need to apply lotion after you bathe, it needs to be one that doesn't dry out too fast because if it is, it won't be long until you are ashy again.

As you go about your day, you come in contact with millions of germs and dirt that you simply cannot see on the surface. The evidence of this can sometimes be found under your finger nails and toe nails. If your finger nails are too long, you risk injuring yourself and even others as you go about your daily routine. If your toe nails are too long, they will tear through your socks, and soon you will develop holes in them.

So as you pay attention to your daily bathing habits, make certain that your finger nails and toe nails are clean, clipped, and free of dirt. There are grooming kits available that give you the opportunity to clean them throughout the day as well.

Brush Your Teeth Daily

Brushing your teeth daily serves two purposes: To clean old food and drinks off of your teeth and to freshen your breath. One of the first things people recognize about you is the color and condition of your teeth and your breath. The color and condition of your teeth says a lot about you, and man to man, most women find it hard to like a man who doesn't take care of his teeth. You can have the best clothes that money can buy, but if your mouth is "jacked up", that usually cancels everything else out.

The dental health experts say that you are to brush your teeth twice a day, as well as floss. By doing this, you prevent the bacteria in your food from turning into a harmful disease in your mouth. However, there are exceptions. Some people suffer with certain sicknesses that affect their dental hygiene, and some people just can't afford to get their teeth corrected by a dentist.

Outside of these kinds of circumstances, there really is no excuse for you not to take care of your oral hygiene. It shows a lack of self-respect when a person neglects to take care of their teeth.

Comb/Brush Your Hair Daily

Brushing and combing your hair should be just as natural as brushing your teeth. You should never leave your house without brushing or combing your hair. Some young men have low-cut fades; others have afros, while others have braids or dreads. Depending on your schedule, you may not be able to make it to the barber or hair stylist every week, but that is not an excuse for you to neglect your hair. If you have braids, try your best to keep them fresh. If you prefer to wear your hair low, make it a priority to brush it throughout the day. If you sport an afro, make sure you keep it trimmed, tapered, and lined up. Regardless of how you wear your hair, it is your responsibility to be on top of your game as it relates to combing or brushing your hair regularly.

Attire

Have you ever judged someone by what they were wearing? You probably don't want to admit it, but I am willing to bet that you've done it at least once in your life. It is not good that people do it, but the truth is that we do. When someone doesn't appear to be dressed to our standards, it becomes easy to judge and then isolate them. Don't be misled. The same way that you judged someone else by their appearance is the same way someone is going to judge you. The word *'judge'* is a strong expression that has several meanings, all of which place another person's opinion of you in front of your opinion of yourself. This is not fair, but it is reality.

If you walk into a room and your clothes are filthy and smelly, people are going to classify you as a bum and they may reject you. If you walk into a room with your pants sagging and your hat cocked to the back, people may classify you as a thug and will treat you as if you're uneducated. A person that walks into a room with a nice, clean suit on is considered to be important and will be treated as such. Honestly, I don't think it's right that one person gets treated better than the other. Who knows, the bum may be the most intelligent person in the room, but because of how he looks, people won't even give him a chance to speak. The thug may be extremely articulate and have the kindest heart, but because of how he presented himself, he may not get the chance to speak or share his kindness. I know how it feels to be treated like this. It has happened to me on several occasions. That is why I can tell you what not to do and how to present yourself.

Don't think that I am asking you to be a "sell out". That is not the message I am trying to convey here, but you must be mindful of how people perceive the way you dress. I, for one, am a firm believer that we all have our own unique style, and I encourage you to express it, but do it in the proper setting. In arenas such as music, fashion, and film, it may be alright to express yourself through your personal style. But in everyday life, you cannot be so stubborn about being original that you position yourself out of a potential life-changing opportunity. A job interview is not the place to wear jeans and jerseys. A business meeting is not the proper setting for a fitted hat and a t-shirt. The way you dress makes you either a player in the game or a spectator. Give yourself a chance to at least play the game.

I have made the choice to always try my best to look professional. Again, I don't think it is fair for people to judge others by their clothes, but I also don't want to give anyone a reason to classify me in the wrong way. I want a fair chance to express my views and perspectives because I believe I have something to say. I want the same opportunities for you as well. Believe that you have the power to control people's perception of you. Give them a chance to get to know you and then provide a value that no one else can provide. Yes, what you wear and how you wear it is very important. My question to you is: What do you want to be perceived as, and will you give yourself a chance to play the game?

LOVE YOUR FAMILY

Outside of loving God and yourself, loving your family is the next important thing. The purpose of family is to provide a support system for your life. When you win, your family is there to celebrate with you. When you lose, your family is there to comfort and console you. There is no earthly substitute for the type of love a family can give. We all like to receive the love and support that our family provides, but what makes family so much more powerful is when we give back the love we receive.

It is so easy to become selfish when you are in a supportive and nurturing environment. As you receive a lot of attention, it can become hard to see what you can give back. That's just human nature; we like to be catered to. However, I encourage you to distribute just as much love as you collect.

Some of you may not even feel love from your family. You may not have the kind of supportive and nurturing environment that I talk about in this book. However, that doesn't mean you have to hold back from showing and sharing your love. Spend some quality time with your younger sibling who looks up to you. Take a few minutes out of your week to visit your grandparent. Tell your mom or dad that you love them without expecting to get something in return. Make sure that the love is genuine and not driven by a selfish motive. Love is free. You should never have to pay to receive it, and you should never make others pay to receive it from you. However, be wise; don't allow anyone to abuse your love, but make sure you show as much love to your family as possible because they need your support just as much as you need theirs.

LOVE YOUR COMMUNITY

Your community is made up of a group of people who believe the same things and apply those beliefs to their everyday lives. Your community can be your neighborhood, your church, your school, your group of friends, or your sports team. Regardless of what type of community you are a part of, the people involved are responsible for how everyone operates inside of that community. They set the rules and guidelines that allow everyone to function in a way that sustains their way of life. The type of community I will talk about in the portion of the book is your physical neighborhood, your place of residence in a particular city.

I have observed that there are several types of communities: communities that enforce rules and regulations that cause them to flourish and thrive, and communities who live by codes that cause them to deteriorate and eventually die.

In communities that flourish and thrive, the people usually have healthier eating habits and their environment is clean and free of clutter and unnecessary trash and garbage. There is a sense of safety that allows its residents to roam freely without fear of danger. They tend to respect one another's values and space as well. These are considered to be "good" communities. The characteristic that I just described is evidence of how the people in that community have made a choice to promote actions that help them to be functional and attractive to those who are considering joining their community.

Communities that deteriorate and eventually die are those that have a lack of respect for one another. They tend to abuse one another, destroy their environment, and have no regard for the safety of those who are a part of their community. Among its residents, there is a constant fear that at any given moment, they can be taken advantage of. The eating habits are poor and living conditions are unfavorable. Given the opportunity, its residents would rather live in a "good" community, but sadly, some of them feel as if they have no choice but to suffer where they are. They feel trapped and believe they have no hope for escaping. If only they knew that they *could* escape if they so desired. I believe that everyone has the power to either change their environment or change their environment. Let me explain.

If you are a participant in a community that is dark, depressing, and cold, you have the power and authority to change the culture of that environment before it destroys itself. You can become the light in the darkness and make a positive impression on the depression by bringing a sense of warmth to the people who are just as affected by the negativity as you are. You can be the change that your community needs to flourish and prosper. All it takes is for you to make a decision to do it.

The other side of the statement means that you have the option to get out of the darkness and move to a community that can help you grow as a person, which allows you to help others grow as well. To use professional sports as an example, have you ever noticed how an athlete struggles on one team and then once he is traded to another team, he plays better? It's kind of like that. Some environments support your growth, while other environments don't. Either option you choose is perfectly fine, but make sure that whatever option you choose, you add to that community instead of draining it.

What actions or deeds cause you to feel loved or appreciated?

_____
_____
_____
_____

In what ways have you shown love to someone else recently? What was their reaction?

_____
_____
_____
_____
_____

How has God shown His love to you?

_____
_____
_____
_____
_____

What aspects of God's love have you applied in your life? How has that affected the way you view the world?

_____
_____
_____
_____
_____

Study the following terms. How would you rate yourself? (Circle the terms that apply to you.)

Boring	Popular	Star Athlete	Ladies Man
Loner	Unpopular	Smart	Handsome
Geek	Nerd	OK	Likeable

Do you love yourself? Why? Why not?

_____
_____
_____
_____
_____

Have you ever been guilty of not bathing, brushing your teeth, or combing your hair? What was your excuse?

_____
_____
_____
_____
_____

How important is it for you to wear clean clothes?

_____
_____
_____
_____
_____

How would you feel if someone didn't give you a chance because of what you were wearing?

_____
_____
_____
_____
_____

As you observe your communities, are you a part of those that are being destroyed or those that are flourishing? Give two examples.

_____
_____
_____
_____
_____

In what ways have you given back to your community? How did you feel after you did it?

_____
_____
_____
_____
_____

WALK LIKE A KING

CHAPTER 2
INTEGRITY

DOING WHAT'S RIGHT

Integrity is a word that we hear all of the time. We associate it with honesty, loyalty, fairness, and justice. It is one of those words that we seem to honor more than most words in the English vocabulary because it has less to do with being a superstar and more to do with being a super person.

A person who has integrity practices doing the right things every chance they get. When you have integrity, you announce that you have taken notice of all things right in the world and you seek to abide by the rules and guidelines of success. It says that you will neglect your selfish nature and commit to treating people with respect at all times, even if that means you cannot get exactly what you want. It means that you will sacrifice your will to win to make sure the game is played fairly.

You can tell if a person has integrity by the choices they make. If you see someone stealing out of a store, more than likely they don't have integrity. If you are in class and your neighbor asks to cheat off of your paper, there is a strong chance they don't have integrity. Some people may feel that these two examples seem petty compared to the bigger crimes that criminals go to prison for. You may believe that we are not perfect and we will make mistakes regularly. You are absolutely correct. We will make mistakes often, but you should always compare your thoughts and actions to what integrity requires at that moment. Unlike a bowl of cereal, you cannot eat integrity. Integrity is not like a lotion you can rub on or a sweet-smelling cologne you can spray on so that others can admire. Integrity is something you live every day. It's something that you are; it is part of your personality. Integrity is something you practice so that it eventually becomes a part of what you are, not just something you do to impress people.

Some of the most successful people in the world live out integrity every day. Business owners, church pastors, teachers, doctors, and athletes all have to practice integrity consistently in order to serve the people who depend on them. Business owners have to make sure they are charging their customers a fair price for their product. Church pastors have to be careful not to use their members' money in a selfish manner. Teachers have to be mindful not to show favoritism. Doctors have to be careful not to purposely misdiagnose a patient's illness, and athletes have to always be mindful to play fair when they compete.

As you can see, having integrity is a serious character trait, but what would happen if these successful people decided to be selfish and ignore the call of integrity? I believe that the world would fall apart and there would be even more tragedies than there have already been. I think it is safe to say that integrity is what holds us together and it is one of the most important character traits that anybody can have.

Below are a few words that promote integrity and they are mixed in with words that are the opposite of integrity. Identify the words that describe you as a person and circle them. After you complete this, answer the questions that follow.

Honest	Love	Truthful	Honor	Good	Pure
Sincere	Righteous	Innocent	Decent		Dishonest
Hate	Unfair	Bad	Corrupt	Cheater	Guilty
Liar	Dishonor	Impure	Polite	Wrong	Best
Worst	Kind	Loyal	Fair	Harsh	Drama	Quiet

What is your definition of integrity?

_____
_____
_____
_____

In what ways have you practiced integrity?

_____
_____
_____
_____
_____

Is it important for you to be truthful even though you may not win? Why?

_____
_____
_____
_____
_____

CHAPTER 3
GOALS

VISION AND ACTION

If you truly desire to walk like a king, you have to set goals. Period. There is no way around it. You cannot maximize your opportunities to walk like a king until you have an idea of what you want out of life. Goals are the end result to what we tenaciously work hard for. We can see evidence of this in the world of sports. A basketball player's main objective is to score baskets. Players run around on hardwood floors with little to no equipment to support them.

They run fast, jump high, and fall hard. Plays are designed to get the ball through the hoop. Players exercise so they have a better chance at scoring and the coaches strategize just so their team can score the most baskets. Hockey players have a similar objective as they skate around on ice for over two hours, slapping around a six-ounce hockey puck, wearing over 20 pounds of equipment. If these athletes risk their lives every day in order to meet a sports goal, how much more important is it for you to dedicate your life to reaching your personal goals?

Without a goal, you become stuck in hopelessness. Your life will resemble the rat running around in the wheel: You put forth a huge amount of energy for no reason, and in return you get nowhere.

Allow me to share with you my process of goal setting. This method has helped me accomplish several of the most important goals in my life. I even wrote this book by using this method so that is a clear indication that it works. I encourage you to read the following paragraphs and begin to form an idea of how you would like to accomplish your goals. Feel free to use my method or you can take bits and pieces of mine to create your own.

KNOW WHAT YOU WANT

Someone once said that if you don't know what you want, someone else will tell you what you want. I think that is one of the saddest places to be in, and I feel bad for the person who is in this position. For someone else to make goals and decisions for you is not a good way to live your life. No one knows you better than *you*. You know what you like and don't like. You know what makes you happy and what makes you sad, so why would you allow someone else to dictate your life?

Knowing what you want out of life starts with having an idea of what you like to do. What productive activities do you enjoy doing more than anything? If you like to draw, you may need to look into art classes. If you like electronics or video games, you may want to explore a career in technology. When I was younger, I loved playing basketball and writing. I made the choice that I loved basketball so much that I wanted to play college basketball, and when I was a senior in high school, I received a basketball scholarship to play in college.

I also enjoyed writing songs and poems. Some of them were good, but I have to admit, there were some that just weren't that good. However, despite having a few bad ones, I kept writing and eventually people started noticing that I had a gift for putting words together nicely. One of those people was my eighth grade language arts teacher, Mrs. Yvonne Ray. She was associated with the NAACP and encouraged me to enter a writing contest that celebrated Black History Month. I wrote how the work of Martin Luther King, Jr. influenced my life, and I won first place.

From that point, I made the decision that I wanted to make writing a priority and hoped that someday, I could make money doing it. However, if I had no idea what I wanted to do in life or was too afraid to use the things that I was good at, I would have never accomplished my writing goals and this book that you are reading right now would have never been written.

PRACTICE FOR POWER

Anybody who wants to be great at anything needs to practice. Some people think that they don't have to practice, but without practice, you never get to reach your full potential. Before Olympic sprinters have the opportunity to run in the Olympics, they have to practice every day for four years straight just to run a race that lasts less than 30 seconds. To be a doctor, you have to go to school for more than eight years in order to have a chance to work as a real doctor. Most criminal lawyers attend school for at least seven years before they get hired at a law firm.

In order to have this type of power, you have to practice. There is no place for laziness when you are working to accomplish goals. Laziness is the enemy to productivity. It places restrictions on your dreams and causes you to lose precious time that you can never get back. You probably run into lazy people every day. They always have their hand out asking for something, but they never want to work for anything. They feel as if their opportunity is going to drop out of the sky and land on the couch that they are sleeping on. Well, they are in for a rude awakening. The knock of opportunity is heard by those who are practicing for power.

Practicing for power means that you know what you want and you work every day to attain your goals. You have identified what needs to be done and you do the necessary task that will cause you to accomplish those things. Anyone who is practicing for power will always be in a good position to receive life-changing opportunities.

CREATE A PERSONAL GOAL SHEET

If there is one thing that helped me to see my dreams come true faster, it was when I created a goal sheet for myself. A goal sheet identifies the goal you want to accomplish and requires you to create meaningful tasks to make sure you reach your goal on purpose. There are three parts to a Personal Goal Sheet: The Goal, The Task, and The Milestone Celebration. The Goal section allows you to list the objective you want to achieve. It serves as the main reason why you are putting in the work in the first place. The Task section outlines the top five assignments that need to be completed in order for the goal to be considered accomplished. The assignments don't have to be done in order, just as long as they get done. You don't have to wait until you complete one in order to move to the next one.

Sometimes, you will be able to complete two assignments at one time. If this opportunity presents itself, feel free to do it. Don't hold back, but be sure to totally complete the task. A halfway completed task cannot be accepted as totally completed. Don't cheat yourself out of developing this winning discipline.

The Milestone Celebration gives you an opportunity to reward yourself for completing your goal. A milestone is a highlight or a high point that has been reached. You can only have a Milestone Celebration once you have completed every task on your goal sheet. Your celebration doesn't have to be something big that costs a lot of money. It can be something small, but make sure it's meaningful to you. When you finally accomplish your goal, you will have enough confidence to fill out another goal sheet and soon, you will have another Milestone Celebration to look forward to.

On the next page is an example of how my Personal Goal Sheet looks. This is what I use whenever I challenge myself with a new goal. I have tried to accomplish goals without it, but I never seem to be successful when I do so. However, every time I follow this Personal Goal Sheet process, I accomplish more, faster. I am convinced that my ambition becomes clearer the more I practice this discipline, and my attitude about my future becomes more positive. You can visit my website (www.WalkLikeAKing.com) to download a copy.

PERSONAL GOAL SHEET

GOAL_____

TASK:
1._____
2._____
3._____
4._____
5._____

MILESTONE CELEBRATION

VISION WALL

Once you have created your goal sheet, find a place in your room where you can hang it up. The wall space that you choose is called your vision wall. A vision wall serves as reminder of the commitment you have made to yourself to be more serious about your future. I am a firm believer that what you see is what you get. So if you have written your goals down and placed them on your bedroom wall, you will be able to look at them whenever you want.

The more you look at what you have accomplished, the more encouraged you will feel about your future. Soon it will become a part of your lifestyle. As time passes, you will be able to add pictures to your goal sheet as well; this is when it starts to get even more real to you. When you are ready to add pictures to your goal sheet, you must look for photos that connect to your goal.

Let's say for instance that one of your goals is to make your school's basketball team. You will look through magazines or print out some pictures from the Internet, cut them out, and fasten them to your goal sheet. You might want to cut out a picture of a basketball, a person shooting a basketball, a basketball goal, or a picture of your favorite basketball player.

Whatever picture you choose, be sure that it connects with your goal so whenever you look at your goal sheet, you don't just see words, but you see pictures as well. For now, let's just stick to the regular goal sheet, and once you've had your first Milestone Celebration, you can add pictures to your next goal sheet.

MEDITATE

Meditation is cool. When you meditate, you get to create your own world where nobody can bother you or distract you from your dreams and goals. You can visualize yourself accomplishing your goals before you ever accomplish them in real life. You literally become your own future for that moment in time.

Meditation gives you the opportunity to block out the commotion of the present world and rest in the success of your future. It provides an escape route to your freedom and a peace that no one else can give.

There are several techniques of meditation, and depending on your flexibility, you can practice a few of them. However, the technique that I use is the chair meditation. To perform the chair meditation, make sure that your environment is quiet and you are sitting in a comfortable position, preferably sitting in a comfortable chair with your feet planted on the ground and your knees bent in an "L" shape. Relax your shoulders and rest your hands on your legs. Gently close your eyes and inhale through your nose, hold your breath for three seconds, and then exhale through your mouth.

Repeat this breathing process three times, and then envision your goals being accomplished. Literally see yourself completing each task and enjoying your Milestone Celebration. If you do this meditation exercise at least three times a week, you will begin to see a difference in how effective you are in accomplishing your goals. I can guarantee you that many young men your age have never made meditation a part of their life. Once you begin to make it a practice, you will notice the difference between you accomplishing your dreams and them accomplishing theirs.

What are the top three goals you want to accomplish in life and why?

_____
_____
_____
_____
_____

Why do you think it is important to practice?

_____
_____
_____
_____
_____

What is the first goal that you are going to put on your goal sheet?

_____
_____
_____
_____
_____

Do you have an area in your room where you can hang your goal sheets? If so, describe that area and why you chose it.

_____
_____
_____
_____
_____

How do you think meditation will help you accomplish your goals faster?

_____
_____
_____
_____
_____
_____

CHAPTER 4

EDUCATION

ACCESS AND POWER

There are many types of education available to you these days. Education is not limited to your school. You can get education in almost any facet of life. Education is nothing more than information offered and used to complete a specific task. A person can get educated on becoming a pilot just as well as they can get educated on becoming a drug dealer. Yes, education can be applied to the perceived good as well as the bad aspects of life. Education crosses all barriers and sees no color; it is there for all to partake of.

However, you must make yourself available to receive the information so that you can exercise it when you need it. When you are educated, you stand out and are recognized as a person who positioned themselves to be prepared for the biggest and best opportunities. Believe me when I say that there are some people who have made the decision not to educate themselves, and they are suffering because of that decision. In the process of life, as I gain more experience, I learn more about people. Through these experiences, I have discovered that there are three types of people who exist in the world: seekers, peekers and neithers.

Seekers are always searching for ways to better themselves. They acquire new information regularly and are full of education. Some seekers even have the ability to educate others on how to become seekers themselves. Seekers are some of the most influential people in the world because they understand the importance of challenging themselves to get better, and as they challenge themselves, the world gets better in the process.

Peekers are people who know how to seek, but are too lazy to do so. They have access to new information and education, but are too afraid to pursue it. They always talk about what they are about to do, but they never follow through. Therefore, they are left uneducated and they never really progress. Peekers have the potential to make a huge impact on the world because they have all the right tools, but they refuse to use them.

Neithers don't care about new information, even though it can help them live a better life; they would rather remain poor and complain about what they don't have instead of working toward improving their life. They have what it takes to do big things, but they are just too lazy.

The seeker, peeker, and neither all have the same choice to make. They must either embrace the new information that has been provided and get educated, or refuse the new information and remain ignorant. You have these same choices available to you as well. You are the only one who controls the amount of knowledge you embrace or reject. There is a world full of new information that can help push you closer to your success, but it is up to you to go get it. It will not just drop in your lap. Resist the feeling to wait until the time is right. That is just an excuse to buy you more time to be mediocre.

Your willingness to endure the studying and the test in order to better yourself places you among the leaders who are changing the world. You have what it takes to use your education to not only enhance the world, but to change the flow of your family. In a world full of seekers, peekers, and neithers, I can sense that you are most definitely a seeker, but the only way to know for sure is to produce the evidence through your actions.

Are you a seeker, peeker, or neither? Explain why. What will you do to improve or maintain your current status?

_____
_____
_____
_____
_____

In what profession do you want to become more educated and why have you chosen that profession?

_____
_____
_____
_____
_____
_____

CHAPTER 5

DETERMINATION

RICO'S STORY

When I was in high school, I had a friend named Rico who ran on our school's track team. Rico was one of the most dedicated athletes that I have ever encountered. He was the first one to practice and the last one to leave. He never missed a track meet, and even when he was injured, he still ran. He never complained about how hard the work was or the sacrifices he had to make in order to be on the team. No matter how he felt, he still competed.

With all of this positive energy in his favor, you would think that he was one of the most elite runners on the team. The truth is that Rico never won a race his entire high school career. When I say never, that is exactly what I mean. He didn't even win a race in practice. There was a time when his competitors felt so bad for him that they would give him their medals and trophies just so he could experience what it felt like to wear one. His four-year losing streak was not a result of him not wanting to win or his lack of effort. The reason he didn't win was because he was born with a physical impairment that caused him to limp when he walked. For that reason, he was unable to compete at a high level. Rico had all of the components of a top-notch track star, except the ability to run effectively. So, no matter how fast or hard he ran, the chances of him winning a race were slim.

Although the people in the stands would laugh at him, he never stopped running. He wasn't embarrassed by the constant losing and the never-ending ridicule. He never complained about the races being unfair or the extreme weakness in his legs. Rico kept doing what he'd always done to prepare for his races; he was determined.

As his friend, I got tired of seeing him lose and decided to approach him about possibly trying another sport. I said, "Rico, why do you continue to show up to practice and the track meets when you know that you're going to lose?" He flashed a smile and said enthusiastically, "If I stop running, I don't have a chance to win. As long as I am running, I have a chance!"

Rico made up in his mind that his determination to win outweighed everyone else's expectation of him to lose. It didn't matter who laughed at him or booed his efforts. It didn't even matter that his friends were embarrassed and tried to convince him to stop running. He knew what he wanted, and that was to someday win a race. Even though it was physically impossible for him to cross the finish line and be declared the first place winner, he still pursued it. In his honor, I have taken the letters of Rico's name and created an acronym to help strengthen your determination. "**R**" stands for Reach Down Deep; "**I**" stands for Ignore The Haters; "**C**" stands for Center Of Confidence; and "**O**" stands for Overcome Obstacles.

REACH DOWN DEEP

I often think about how Rico continued to press through his setbacks, and did it with so much passion. Why would a guy who knew that he could never win keep pressing toward the finish line? They only sensible answer I can conjure up is that he had something inside of him that kept running, even though the world thought that he should lie down and quit. He possessed an unyielding will to finish, even though he knew his chances at meeting the world's standards of winning were non-existent.

It's funny how life can tease us sometimes. We will have mountain-top experiences but then, when we least expect it, life can throw us speeding curve balls that dare us to adjust or get hit. Rico definitely had a curve ball thrown his way, but never once did I hear him complain about his lot. All he cared about was being the best that he could be for that moment in time, and every day he would reach down deep to find the strength to compete the best way he knew how--mentally and physically.

I believe that the only way a person can be totally comfortable with their results is if they know they have done everything they could have done to be the best they could have been for that moment. When you know that you have given it your all, and there is nothing more you can do, you have to find it in your heart to believe that and own your work. Sometimes, in order to have peace about your disposition, you have to access a strength that can only be found deep within your soul, and this strength will help build your character as you face other obstacles in life. Trust me; there will be other obstacles.

IGNORE THE HATERS

I have a confession to make. I am a closet rebel. Not a rebel in the sense of causing unnecessary trouble, but a rebel in the sense that I hate being labeled. I have never been fond of being put in a box; I believe that it limits my ability to stretch beyond other people's expectations. Even though I hate being pegged, I have learned that in order to deal with people on a civilized level, you have to know their tendencies. The more you deal with people, the better you become with understanding their energy and the easier it becomes for you to deal with them. So with that said, I will introduce three types of *people energy* to you: promoters, passives, and detractors.

PROMOTERS

Promoters are people who love you no matter what. They know your heart and are loyal to your causes. They are what I like to call "pillars" as they willfully hold you up and stand firm in your corner. Promoters can be trusted in more ways than one; these types of people draw attention to your positive characteristics and help you mature in the areas you need to work on without making you feel like less of a person. They skillfully handle you with grace and love.

Whenever you need advice or guidance, you can count on the promoter to help you through it. They are what Tupac Shakur called "ride or die". They are totally committed to seeing you succeed, even if means they have to sacrifice their extra time, energy, and resources to make sure it happens. They love you just as much as they love themselves.

PASSIVES

Passives are the people in your life that can go either way. They are annoyingly fickle, can change on you at the drop of dime, and are dreadfully inconsistent. As long as you are scratching their backs, they will remain by your side. But as soon as they sense that they no longer have your attention, they begin to get antsy and they will turn their backs on you. They are real good at being your friend when they can get something from you.

They pretend to support you, but they are really looking for an opportunity to make themselves look better. The way to figure out who your passive friends are is to see who is still around when you are in a bad situation. Passive people usually don't call to check on you and they don't offer to help you without expecting something in return. Be careful of how much information you tell them because they have the tendency to use that information against you when they get upset or feel rejected by you.

DETRACTOR

Lastly, there is the detractor. This is the same type of person who is a hater. A hater is someone whose only motive is to prevent you from progressing, they have no real reason not to like you, and they simply refuse to like you just because. Nothing that you do pleases them and probably never will. They are not happy with themselves, so how can they truly be happy with you?

We all need promoters and at times, we can probably even tolerate the passives, but the detractor is the one you want to ignore completely. There is no way to get them on your side, so don't waste your energy trying to persuade them because they will distract you from seeing the big picture. You are a child of God who has access to a life that is both quality and meaningful, and the seed to your destiny has already been planted inside of you. However, when the detractor is around, you will get tangled up in their web of complaining, frustration, and detailed negativity. Detractors are energy consumers. The more energy you give them, the more energy they want. They thrive on drama!

CENTER OF CONFIDENCE

Put yourself in Rico's shoes, if you will. The chances of you being recognized as a champion are slim to none. You never had the chance to cross the finish line with the rest of your team, and you have been stricken with a physical ailment that is irreversible. You have a losing hand. What do you do?

Do you cry and complain about the unfairness? Do you ask your coach to change your workout so that you can feel like you are keeping up with the rest of your teammates? Do you ask those whom you are competing against to slow down so that you can keep up? Not if you're Rico, you don't.

Rico found his center of confidence and that is what allowed him to keep his focus on the track. He didn't find his center of confidence at practice or on the track. He found it within himself. When he shared with me that the only way he had a chance to win was to keep running, that let me know that his center of confidence was internal. It was something he gained away from the action. Yes, people did congratulate him on his efforts and he even found joy when we would cheer him on, but I truly believe that no matter if he had people cheering or jeering, his mind was already set on completing his task. His center of confidence would not allow his motivation to be swayed.

Distractions are minimized when you have a center of confidence. You are not easily shaken when you have a center of confidence. It becomes difficult for you to stay depressed for long periods of time when you have a center of confidence.

One thing you can learn from Rico is that in order to commit yourself totally to being a king, you must find your center of confidence. The center of confidence is that place where you experience peace no matter what is going on. Your past success and accomplishments are there, and the walls are covered with your moral trophies and plaques. You understand that you have prepared yourself for this specific moment. You have done your stretches and jumping jacks, and the only thing that is in front of you now is the finish line.

You don't care if the person next to you looks bigger and stronger than you do, or if you are running in an unfamiliar territory. There is no way that you will allow external elements to disrupt your internal hope. You have found your center of confidence, and you will use that as your energy until you cross the finish line.

OVERCOME OBSTACLES

Every so often, I have the privilege of meeting a person who has overcome extraordinary challenges. These individuals usually possess the kind of strength and motivation that can move mountains. When I encounter these types of people, I classify them as a go-getter. Life will continue to bring you headache, heartache, struggle, and gloom; however, you can overcome those challenges, and that is what separates the go-getters from the no-getters.

If a go-getter is a person who overcomes obstacles and doesn't stop until they reach the finish line, a no-getter is someone who talks about winning, but never even gets in position to start the race. A go-getter is someone who sees the hurdles and figures out a way to clear them, but a no-getter sees the hurdles and decides to wait until the wind knocks the hurdles down, which will probably never happen.

A go-getter is the one who is mentally prepared for whatever may happen, while a no-getter is the one who watches everyone else stretch and warm up, and yet thinks he can compete on pure talent alone. The main difference between these two types of people is this: Go-getters aren't afraid to get started, while no-getters wait for something to happen so that they can get started. As one who has been chosen to lead others, you simply cannot be afraid of the challenges. There will always be something standing between you and the finish line, be it fatigue, another competitor, the weather, or injury, but you have to have the resolve to overcome those things. Learning how to conquer the world requires you to reach down deep, capture the will to ignore the detractors, and find your center of peace. Once you embrace these principles, you will be able to overcome any challenge set before you and triumph in any situation. You are a go-getter, so go get it!

Ignore the detractor, keep your eyes on the passives, and celebrate your promoters often. Don't give place to anything that has the power to derail you from staying on track. Your determination will help you achieve goals that others thought you could never achieve; it provides opportunities that money could never provide. Others will be able to look at your life and be inspired to do their best, as well. Your decision to stay determined can impact people you will never meet, just like Rico's determination has impacted your life today.

What lessons did you learn from Rico's story?

_____
_____
_____
_____
_____
_____

On a scale of 1 to 10, how would you rate your determination toward reaching your life goals? How will you improve from this day forward?

_____
_____
_____
_____
_____

Would you consider yourself to be a go-getter? Why? Why not?

_____
_____
_____
_____
_____

Can you identify the detractors in your life? Who and what are they?

_____

_____

_____

_____

_____

_____

CHAPTER 6
PERSISTENCE
DON'T STOP UNTIL YOU WIN

Persistence is the cousin to determination; you can't have one without the other. If determination means that you have made up in your mind that you will not quit until you've reached your goal, persistence is what allows you to stay focused on your goal, despite the challenges that may arise.

Persistence causes you to look past your present status and press toward the next level of your success. When your emotions try to stop you from moving forward, persistence causes you to readjust your attitude so that you can move forward with confidence. If your past failures try to terrorize your mind, you can arm yourself with persistence and counterattack the discomfort of those past memories.

When you are persistent, you disregard the opinions of those who have no real say or control over your life because you can see further into your future than they can. Because you have established your love for God, yourself, family, and your community, you understand who is for you and who is against you. You have written down your goals and have invested in getting more education so that you can see which direction you need to travel in. Your determination is at a level that cannot be stopped, and your focus will not be shaken. Once you've reached this point, you become like a thoroughbred horse in the Kentucky Derby.

If you have ever watched a Kentucky Derby race, then you have noticed that the horses have black covers over their eyes. Those covers are called "blinders". The purpose of the blinders is to make sure that the horse doesn't get distracted by everything else around it. The blinders shield the horse's eyes from looking to the left, right, and backward. The only direction the blinders allow the horse to look is straight ahead toward the finish line. This is what perseverance can do for you. It can help you stay focused on the goals at hand despite your surroundings.

Persistence is more than an emotion; it is a part of your soul that you have to continually access. It only appears when you make it appear. You have the option to be lazy or persistent, and these options will always fight for your attention. Keep in mind that lazy seeds produce lazy fruit, and persistent seeds produce a life of accomplished goals.

There is a story about two friends named Chad and Randy. They were always competing against each other in some way or another. Whether they were playing chess, scrabble, or basketball, neither one wanted to lose to the other. One day, Chad bet Randy that he could make the honor roll before Randy could, and of course, Randy gladly accepted the challenge. Both of them were two of the smartest kids in their class and performed at a high level consistently, but neither of them had ever achieved honor roll status before. During the first week of the contest, both friends performed evenly, getting A's on every assignment, including homework. However, after about a month, Chad's grade point average began to fall. He was no longer making A's on his tests and homework assignments. He was having trouble understanding his work, but he never asked his teachers for help. After a while, he just accepted his grades as they were and figured that he had more than enough time to improve them.

Randy wasn't doing so well either. Just like Chad, his test scores were not good. Seeing that he needed help, he arranged to spend extra time after school with a tutor so that he could improve his grade, and he asked his teachers for practice assignments so that he could become even more familiar with his work. By going the extra mile, this signaled to his teachers that he was serious about developing into a better student.

There were times when Randy didn't want to study or do extra assignments, but because of his desire to make the honor roll, he kept pushing. He even got distracted a few times whenever his favorite show was airing on television, but he remained focused on his goal.

When the end of the marking period arrived, both Chad and Randy received their report cards. As Chad ripped open his white envelope, his face dropped to the floor like a sack of potatoes. He not only didn't make the honor roll, but his report was the worst he had ever received. Now, it was Randy's turn. As he peeled back the folds of his envelope, his face lit up like the sun. He screamed, "I made the honor roll!" His hard work and diligence had paid off. All of those long nights, after school tutoring sessions, and sacrifices caused him to reach his goal. Now, he understood what it meant to be persistent and the importance of staying adamant about pursuing something that he desired.

As you walk like a king, persistence needs to be one of the biggest jewels in your crown. Keep it polished and never let it fall out of its setting. Without persistence, you have no real support for your journey toward conquering the world.

Do you find it hard to be persistent? Why? Why not?

_____
_____
_____
_____
_____

How can persistence help you accomplish your goals?

_____
_____
_____
_____
_____

Do you think it is important to put your blinders on as you work to be successful? Why? Why not?

_____
_____
_____
_____
_____

What are some of the distractions that cause you to push your responsibilities to the side?

_____
_____
_____
_____
_____

CHAPTER 7
SELF CONTROL

MIND OVER MATTER

Self control is probably the most important characteristic that a king can own. With it, unheralded men have experienced great notoriety and success. Without it, men of great stature, fame, and God-like status have been decreased to almost nothing and dismissed as regular.

Not too long ago, I had the opportunity to talk to a group of young men about the importance of self control and how lives can be destroyed because of the lack of it. Our conversation touched on several areas of life that require extreme self control: sex, physical confrontations, parental discipline, and peer pressure. These all are hot topics among young men your age.

I can remember being impacted by these same issues when I was your age, so I was interested to see how self control played a part in these young men's lives as well. Talking about these issues can sometimes be uncomfortable, so I decided to start the conversation by asking a few choice questions that would help spark some excitement and participation. These are the questions I asked:

1. Do you feel like you are under extreme pressure to protect your manhood? Why?

2. Do you find it hard to respect the authority of your parents? Why? Why not?

3. How has peer pressure caused you to make choices that you probably wouldn't have made had you not been pressured?

4. Do sexual pressures cause you to forget about your self control?

5. What does self control mean to you?

I posed these questions because there are countless young men who have never even thought to ask themselves these types of questions, yet they are active citizens in their environment. They could even be some of your friends and family members. I want you to think about how you would answer these questions based on your own experience because at the end of this chapter, you are going to have the opportunity to answer them for yourself.

Self control is an attribute that must be exercised openly and continuously because there are many forces that have the potential to throw you off at any given time. As a king, there is a level of awareness that you must have at all times. This awareness will help you find a way to avoid making the wrong choices as it relates to issues such as these.

As a young man practicing self control, you are in charge of your own emotions, desires, urges, and reactions. The power is always in your hands to make the right decisions and when you relinquish that power to an outside source, whether it is a person or a substance, it diminishes your ability to function properly and you lose the respect of those you come in contact with. The basis of self control is integrity, knowing what's right and wrong, and having enough courage to make the right choices even when the wrong choices are stronger at the moment.

People have lost their lives because of the lack of self control. Young girls have gotten pregnant and young boys have become fathers because of the lack of self control. Self control is not something you are born with; it is a character trait you have to develop through practice and give consistent attention to performing regularly. You cannot allow your pride to intercept your efforts to expand your borders of self control.

A young man of your caliber is expected to be the example of all things positive; you should be the poster child for self control and the template for other young men. Your manhood has nothing to do with how many women you sleep with or the number of dudes you knock out. Being disrespectful to your parents is not the way to gain their respect or trust, and allowing your friends to lead you into trouble only makes you a mindless follower.

Please hear me when I say this young king: recognize who you are and the impact that you have on this world. Practice self control on a daily basis, because a person in your position has a wealth of influence over your generation and the generations following you.

Do you believe having self control is difficult? Why?

_____
_____
_____
_____
_____

Do you feel like you are under extreme pressure to protect your manhood? Why?

_____
_____
_____
_____
_____

Do you find it hard to respect the authority of your parents?

_____
_____
_____
_____
_____

How has peer pressure caused you to make choices that you probably wouldn't have made had you not been pressured?

_____
_____
_____
_____
_____

Do sexual pressures cause you to forget about your self control?

_____
_____
_____
_____
_____

What does self control mean to you?

_____
_____
_____
_____
_____

CHAPTER 8
K.I.N.G

WHAT IT ALL MEANS

If you are reading this, you have made it to the end of this book. Congratulations for completing the Walk Like A King Challenge, but the party doesn't stop now. You have just started to dance. Remember, once you complete one goal, take time to celebrate, but then start working on another goal immediately. You have invested precious time into your own personal development, but the next step is for you to invest in someone else. That is what K.I.N.G. stands for: **K**eep **I**nvesting in the **N**ext **G**eneration.

There have been times where I have made mistakes that I probably didn't have to make. Many of which, I blame myself for and others I blame on not having the foreknowledge that I needed to make better decisions. The only way to get the foreknowledge is to be told about it by someone who has already experienced it. Once you have the knowledge, it is up to you to apply that knowledge. As soon as you have applied it, it then becomes wisdom. Because you have committed to reading this book and have answered the questions, you now have knowledge that many young men your age don't have. Use this knowledge in your everyday life so that when you do share it with someone, it is actually something you have experienced for yourself.

Wisdom is knowledge that has been tested, and with the test comes an experience. Once you experience something, only then can you have true wisdom about it and make better choices in the future. Again, I take full responsibility for the bad choices that I have made in life; no one forced me to make those decisions. However, had someone taken the time to guide me through those certain events, I probably would have made better choices.

You have the power to be a guide to someone else. Keep investing in the next generation because the lessons you learn today will be the wisdom you pass on tomorrow. You must never hold good information all to yourself. You may have the answer to someone else's problem, just like this book may have had an answer to a few of yours. I promise you, there will be someone who could use the knowledge that you have obtained and you will have to make the decision to either deny them that knowledge or distribute it to them. My hope is that you do as I have done and share as much as you can. You could possibly be saving a life, or better yet, saving a generation.

What is the most important lesson you have learned from this book?

_____
_____
_____
_____
_____

How do you plan on sharing the information that you have learned from this book?

_____
_____
_____
_____
_____

Will you recommend this book to someone else? Why?

_____
_____
_____
_____
_____

Of all the lessons you've learned from this book, which one are you going to apply immediately?

_____
_____
_____
_____
_____

Do you see yourself as a king? Why? Why not?

_____
_____
_____
_____
_____
_____
_____
_____
_____
_____

WALK LIKE A KING

CONCLUSION

I believe that you can do anything you set your mind to. If I thought otherwise, I wouldn't have written this book for you. This alone should be an indication of how serious I am about *your* life. My desire is for you to value your life just as much as I do. Don't think that you have forever to live because you don't. Every moment has significance and every second contains a power that could change your life forever. I often tell my students that you only have one life to live, and you can't go to Kmart to put another one on lay-a-way. This can be viewed as comical, but there is so much truth to it. Young man, as you walk like a king, make every moment count and provide the world with a value that can never again be duplicate.

ABOUT THE AUTHOR

"A refreshing voice in today's climate, Jesse A. Cole, Jr. is a leader … for today's generation." For more than a decade, his youth mentoring experience has helped others take a personal inventory of their lives as they engage their hearts toward discovering and walking in their purpose. He earned his undergraduate degree in Communications from Bluefield College and is also an alumni of Kids Across America (KAA) where he worked as a Youth Counselor, Activities Instructor, Basketball Coach and Worship Leader for their outreach program in Golden, MO. He is the CEO of the spiritual development company, Maximize Your Greatness, and is quickly and effectively building a catalogue of successes as an author, seminar presenter/organizer, executive producer, and speaker. With such a high caliber of experience, Jesse A. Cole, Jr. is most definitely one of the rising stars in destiny-driven communication. To book Jesse for your next event, please visit: www.JesseSpeaks.com

"What you want to become depends on your willingness to become it."

"In order to attract the energy you desire, you must project the value that is required for your environment."

"Be careful of always pursuing the sun; you might get blinded by your own ambition."

"When you don't understand how much God loves you, you will look at giving back as a loss instead of a blessing."

"Your power is in what you produce,
not what you portray."

"You can't apply a C-Level commitment to an A-Level endeavor."

"Once you connect your purpose to your passion, you will begin to see each day as a new opportunity to add another piece to your purpose puzzle."

List the top three lessons you learned from this book?

1.

2.

3.

How will you apply these lessons to your life?

_____
_____
_____
_____
_____
_____
_____
_____
_____
_____

DOWNLOAD YOUR FREE WALK LIKE A KING SOUNDTRACK

@ www.WalkLikeAKing.com

FOLLOW ME.

/JesseSpeaks   @JesseSpeaks

THANK YOU FOR YOUR SUPPORT!

WALK LIKE A KING

WALK LIKE A KING

WALK LIKE A KING

WALK LIKE A KING

www.ingramcontent.com/pod-product-compliance
Lightning Source LLC
Chambersburg PA
CBHW071725040426
42446CB00011B/2217